CLARKSON, Stephanie

First published by
Carlton Books Limited 2012
Manufactured under license
by Carlton Books Limited
Text and design copyright
© Carlton Books Limited 2012

Carlton Books Limited,
20 Mortimer Street, London, W1T 3JW.

A CIP catalogue record for this book is
available from the British Library.

10 9 8 7 6 5 4 3 2 1

ISBN: 978-1-84732-645-4

FSC
www.fsc.org
MIX
Paper from
responsible sources
FSC® C101537

Author: Stephanie Clarkson
Executive Editor: Barry Timms
Art Editor: Emily Clarke
Designer: Andy Archer
Cover designer: Emily Clarke
Production: Maria Petalidou

Printed in China

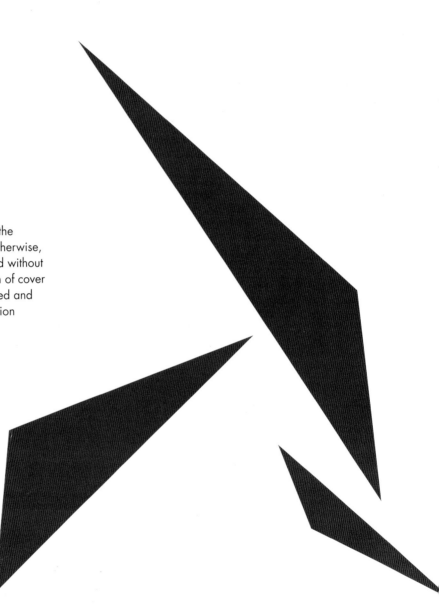

Let's get moving with Wenlock and Mandeville!

CARLTON
BOOKS

Mandeville and Wenlock

Hello sports stars!

We're Wenlock and Mandeville, mascots of the London 2012 Olympic and Paralympic Games. We can't wait to show you the amazing sports you'll see there…

Are you ready to run, jump and ride into action, just like the Olympians and Paralympians?

Let's get moving!

Great to meet you! I'm Grandpa George.

I'm Grandma

My name is Lily

And I'm Jack

Grandpa George made Wenlock and Mandeville from metal used for the Olympic Stadium!

See Mandeville run!

I am running. I pump my arms and move my legs as fast as I can.

Mandeville sprints towards the finish line.

Your turn to run...

I bet you can run really fast! Can you play chase with your friends? Or run after your ball?

Lots of sports involve running...

Football • Hockey • Athletics

Wenlock runs and dribbles the hockey ball.

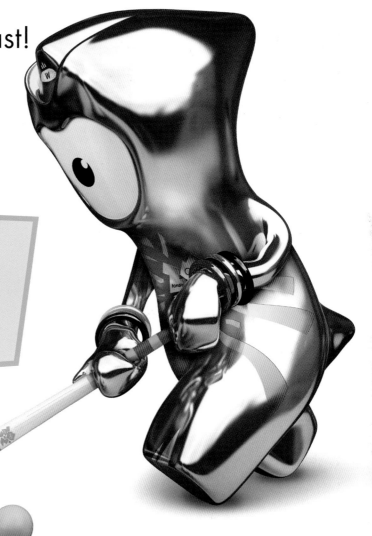

See Wenlock lift!

I am lifting weights. I bend
my knees, keep my back
straight and use my
strong arms.

Wenlock lifts
the heavy bar.

Your turn to lift...

You are already brilliant at lifting. You lift up plastic bricks to build a tower. You lift a cup to your mouth.

Some lifting sports...

Powerlifting • Weightlifting
Judo • Wrestling • Gymnastics

In Judo, players try to lift each other off the ground.

See Mandeville throw!

I am throwing. I hold the ball steady and then launch it up into the air.

Pass to me, Mandeville!

Mandeville practises with Mandip Sehmi. Mandip plays Wheelchair Rugby in the Paralympic Games. He catches the ball, then throws it over the goal line to score.

Mandip Sehmi

Birthday: 13 December 1980

Started playing: Aged 20

Fun fact: Mandip has won two European gold medals.

Your turn to throw...

Throwing is great fun outdoors. See how far you can throw a ball. Can you throw and catch with a friend?

Mandeville is getting ready to throw the basketball into the net.

Here are some other throwing sports...

Basketball • Boccia • Athletics Handball

Wenlock throws the water polo ball across the pool ...

... and runs up to throw the javelin.

See Wenlock stretch and bend!

I stand at the top of the highest board. I stretch up tall on my tiptoes ...

... then bend back to dive into the water.

Well done, Wenlock!

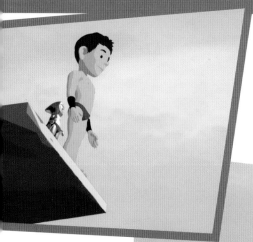

Wenlock loves to dive with Tom Daley. Tom stands on the edge of the board. He springs high into the air and then tumbles over and over.

Ready ...

bend and roll ...

Tom Daley

Birthday: 21 May 1994

Started diving: Aged 7

Fun fact: Tom is the youngest ever British World Champion in any sport!

... splash!

Your turn to stretch and bend...

You stretch when you get out of bed in the morning. You bend down to pick up a toy.

Mandeville stretches to hit the ball ...

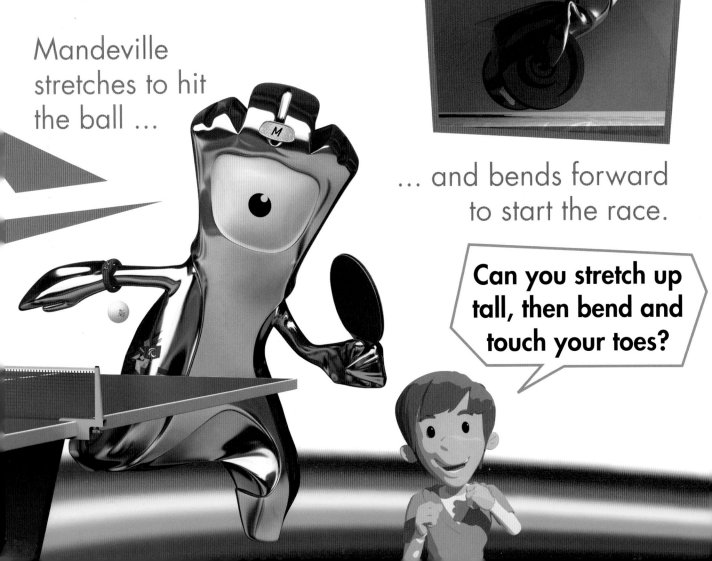

... and bends forward to start the race.

Can you stretch up tall, then bend and touch your toes?

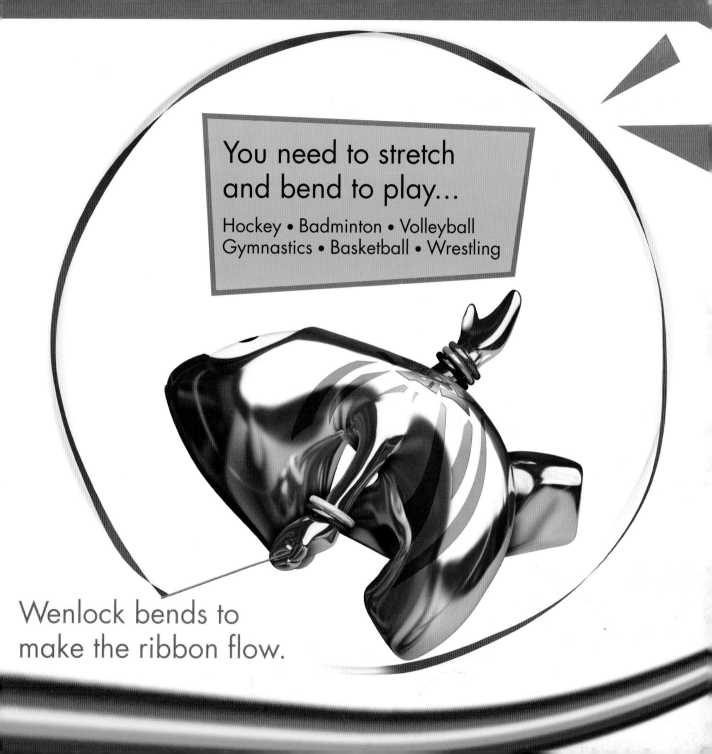

You need to stretch and bend to play...

Hockey • Badminton • Volleyball
Gymnastics • Basketball • Wrestling

Wenlock bends to make the ribbon flow.

I am riding my bike. I look straight ahead, steer with the handlebars and peddle my feet round and round.

Can you ride a bike, tricycle or scooter? Maybe you ride a horse?

The whole family thinks Shanaze Reade is amazing! She rides a BMX around the racetrack, jumping high into the air.

Shanaze Reade

Birthday: 23 September 1988

Started riding: Aged 10

Fun fact: Before BMX became an Olympic event, Shanaze wanted to be a teacher.

See Mandeville pull!

I am practising Archery.
I pull the bowstring back.
Whizzz! The arrow
flies through the air.

Mandeville holds
the bow, pulls and
takes aim.

**You've hit
the gold!**

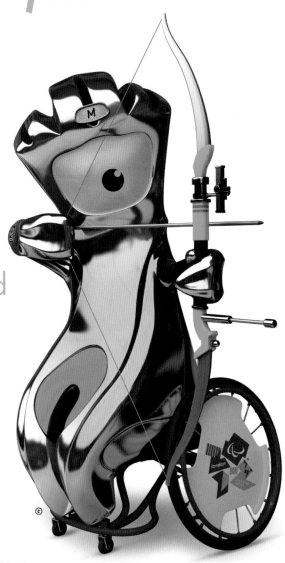

Your turn to pull...

Guess what! You already pull things every day. You pull open a door. You pull on your wellies and you pull the string of your kite.

Wenlock pulls hard on the paddle.

See Wenlock jump!

I am jumping. I bend my knees, straighten my legs, then push on my feet and spring high into the air.

Wenlock jumps across the sand to hit the beach volleyball.

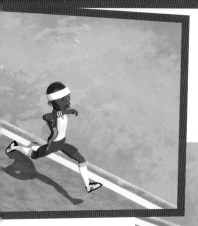

Wenlock loves watching Phillips Idowu practise the Triple Jump! Phillips runs, hops, steps and then jumps high and far.

Run ...

jump ...

... land!

Phillips Idowu

Birthday: 30 December 1978

Started jumping: At school

Fun fact: Phillips loved playing American football and basketball at school.

Your turn to jump...

You jump when you play leap-frog or hopscotch. You jump up and down on your bed.

On a trampoline, you can jump really high.

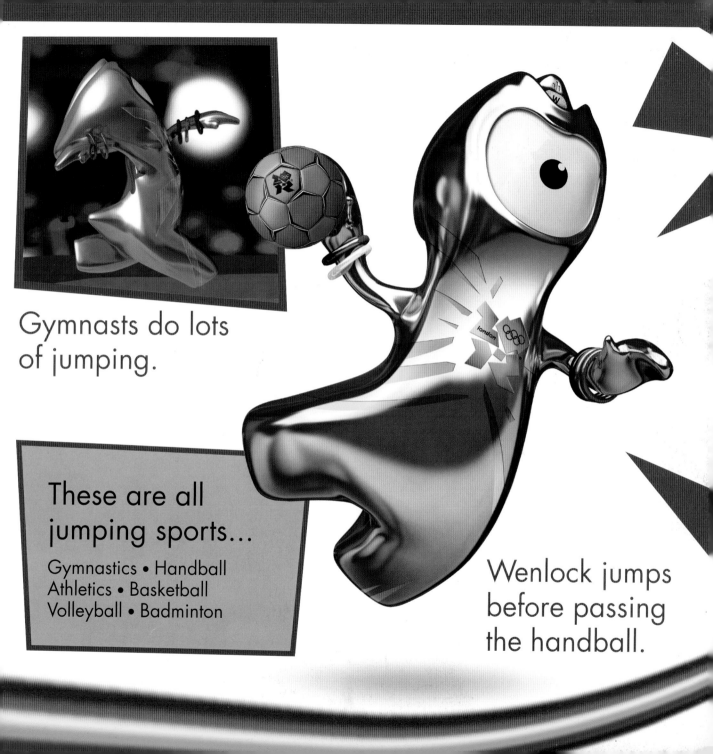

Gymnasts do lots
of jumping.

These are all
jumping sports...

Gymnastics • Handball
Athletics • Basketball
Volleyball • Badminton

Wenlock jumps
before passing
the handball.

See Mandeville kick!

I am playing Football.
I pull my knee back,
straighten my leg
and then ...

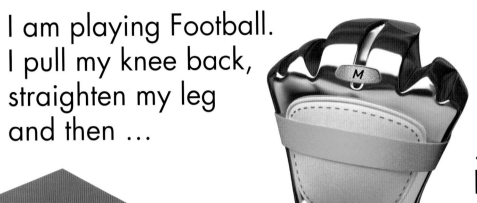

... thwack! I
kick the ball.

There are all kinds
of kicking sports...

Football • Swimming
Taekwondo • Gymnastics

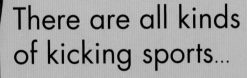

Your turn to kick...

How far can you kick your football? Can you kick your leg high when you dance?

In Taekwondo, players learn special kicking moves.

Remember! You never kick people, unless you are doing martial arts.

See Wenlock balance!

I am balancing on the beam.
This is a tricky handstand, but
I can also balance on my feet.

Wenlock balances
his weight carefully.

**Most sports
involve balance.**

You use your balance to dance, to ride a bike or to stand on one foot.

You need good balance to sail a boat ...

... and ride a tandem.

See Mandeville swim!

I am swimming. I stretch my body out in the water, kick my legs and move my arms like a windmill.

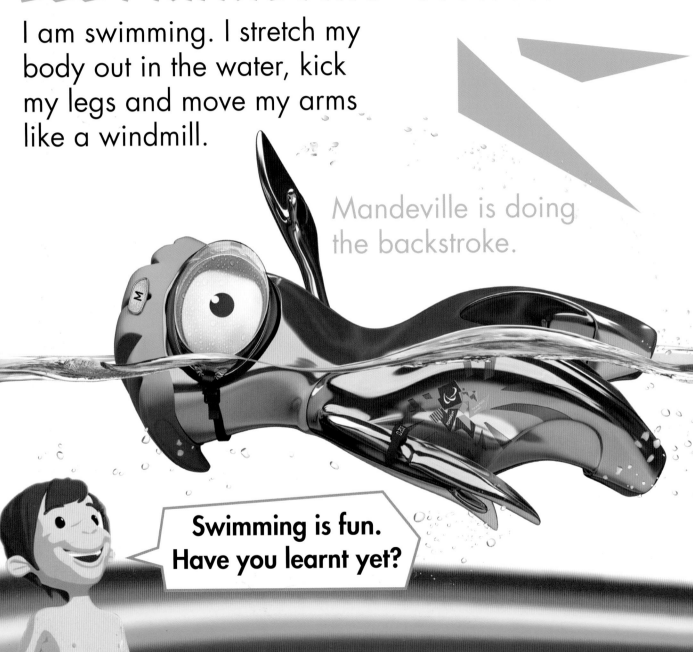

Mandeville is doing the backstroke.

Swimming is fun. Have you learnt yet?

Mandeville loves to swim with Ellie Simmonds. Ellie moves super-fast up and down the pool in her Paralympic races.

Ellie Simmonds

Birthday: 11 November 1994

Started swimming: Aged 5

Fun fact: She is the youngest person ever to have received an MBE medal from Her Majesty the Queen.

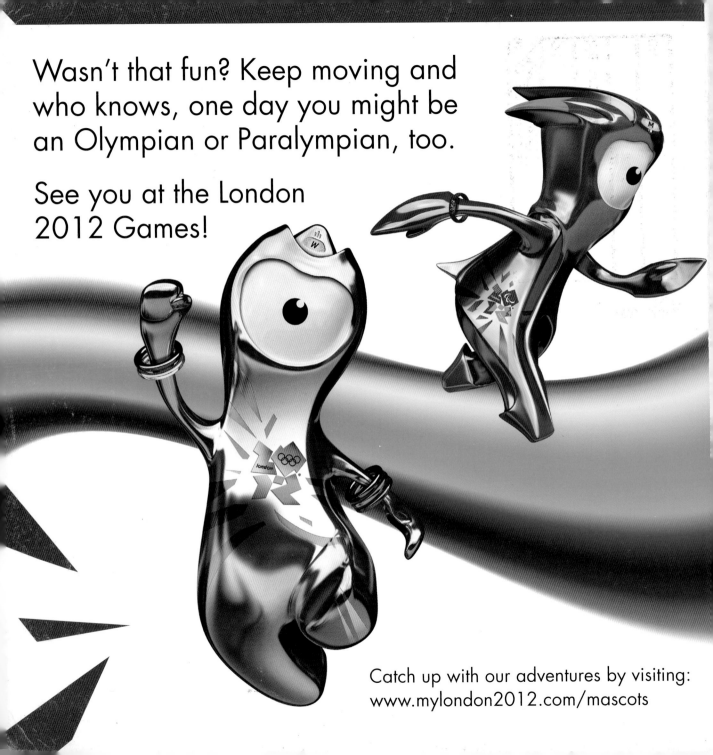

Wasn't that fun? Keep moving and who knows, one day you might be an Olympian or Paralympian, too.

See you at the London 2012 Games!

Catch up with our adventures by visiting:
www.mylondon2012.com/mascots